GET OUT OF YOUR HEAD

LEADER'S GUIDE

JENNIE ALLEN

THOMAS NELSON
Since 1798

Get Out of Your Head Leader's Guide
© 2020 by Jennie Allen

Published in Nashville, Tennessee, by Nelson Books. Nelson Books is a registered trademark of HarperCollins Christian Publishing, Inc.

Based on the book *Get Out of Your Head* by Jennie Allen, © 2020 by Jennie Allen. Used by permission of WaterBrook Publishing, 10807 New Allegiance Drive #500, Colorado Springs, CO 80921.

Typesetting: CrosslinCreative.net

Thomas Nelson titles may be purchased in bulk for educational, business, fundraising, or sales promotional use. For information, please e-mail SpecialMarkets@ThomasNelson.com.

ISBN 978-0-310-11640-0 (softcover)
ISBN 978-0-310-12243-2 (ebook)

First Printing January 2020 / Printed in the United States of America

CONTENTS

INTRODUCTION

Leaders,

I am excited to partner with you in your efforts to pour into the lives of women! I pray that these few short pages will help to equip and prepare you to lead this study. Many of you may have led plenty of groups in the past, or perhaps this is the first you've led. Whichever the case, this is a spiritual calling and you are entering spiritual places with these women—and spiritual callings and places need spiritual power.

My husband, Zac, always says, "Changed lives change lives." If you are not first aware of your own need for life change, the women around you won't see their need. If you allow God into the inner struggles of your heart, the women following you will be much more likely to let Him into theirs. These women do not need to see bright and shiny, perfectly poised people, they need to see people who are a mess and daily dependent on God for their hope and strength.

The apostle Paul actually believed God and he lived like it. And I think as a generation of women, we are longing for the same lives. We want to have strong minds and thoughts—and to believe God is real and to live like it.

This is not a study for people wanting to keep the status quo. This study messes with you because it shows us how to change our thought patterns and live with freedom from the emotional spirals that suck us down. I want a life like Paul's, who had the mind of Christ. I want to run like he did with a clear, disciplined mind, and ultimately with peace.

Together, we can do this. We can and we will encourage one another, hold each other accountable, and break into each other's spirals to keep our focus individually and collectively on Jesus. That is where we will find true freedom. Minds set free come from minds set on Him. We are not bound by this world and we do have power! Let's take control of our minds and stop the spirals.

Jennie

WHAT'S IN THE BOX

Each *Get Out of Your Head* kit includes:

See. A DVD with six sessions

Study. A copy of the Study Guide (each member of your group will need her own study guide). Additional Study Guides can be purchased separately (ISBN: 978-0-310-11637-0).

Lead. A copy of the Leader's Guide

Ask. A set of Conversation Cards

If you have a large group of women and need to break down into smaller groups during your study times, you may want to purchase additional kits so each group can have access to a leader's guide and a set of conversation cards.

We will discuss how to use each element of this kit on pages 12–15.

THE VISION

1. That we would come to realize that the greatest spiritual battle of our generation is being fought between our ears. We have a choice to set our minds on sin and death or life and peace.

> We destroy arguments and every lofty opinion raised against the knowledge of God, and take every thought captive to obey Christ (2 Corinthians 10:5).

2. That we would see that God gave us a choice. We can choose to believe the truth of God's Word rather than the lies of the enemy, and we can choose to interrupt the chaos of our minds. We get to choose moment by moment what we live for.

> Finally, brothers, whatever is true, whatever is honorable, whatever is just, whatever is pure, whatever is lovely, whatever is commendable, if there is any excellence, if there is any worth of praise, think about these things (Philippians 4:8).

3. That women would believe our focus on Christ changes our behaviors and the more we stop believing lies, the more we will live like Him. The rest of this leader's guide is aimed at equipping you to point the women of your group to God in ways that will change their minds, their thoughts, and ultimately their lives.

> Let this mind be in you which was also in Christ Jesus, who, being in the form of God, did not consider it robbery to be equal with God, but made Himself of no reputation, taking the form of a bondservant, *and* coming in the likeness of men (Philippians 2:5–7 NKJV).

PREPARING YOURSELF TO LEAD A GROUP

1. **Pray:** Pray like the world is ending, pray like this is the last chance for people to know Him, pray like our lives and futures depend on it, pray like the future of souls in heaven is at stake. . . . Pray like you need God.

   Pray for your women:

   ▶ That God would show them the ways they need to get out of their own heads.

   ▶ That they would feel safe to open up and process.

   ▶ That they would want more of God and that God would meet them.

   ▶ That the conversation would be focused on God.

   ▶ That we would be humble displays of God's grace to these women.

   ▶ That God would come and fall on your time together.

   ▶ That many would come to a saving faith as they see God for who He is.

2. **Lean on God:** Allow the Holy Spirit to lead every moment together. We have provided you with tools that we will discuss in the next section; however, they are only tools to use as the Spirit leads you and your time together. God will have unique agendas for each of your groups as you depend on Him. Lean into your own weakness and into His strength and direction.

When Jesus left His disciples to go back to His Father in heaven, He said, "Don't go anywhere until you have the helper I will send you." We need to obey that same command. We don't begin until it is with the power of the Holy Spirit within us (see Acts 1:4–5). He is real and available and waiting to flood our lives and the lives around us as we serve and speak. But we have to wait for Him to speak, ask if we should speak and what we should speak, and ask what to do in different situations. God wants us to need Him and to depend on His Spirit. If this is not how you live on a daily basis, begin today.

3. **Be transparent:** If you choose not to be vulnerable, no one else will be vulnerable either. If you desire women to feel safe with you and your group, be vulnerable. This is not an optional assignment. This is your calling as you lead these women.

4. **Listen but also lead:** Listen as women share struggles. Some women are taking a tremendous risk in being vulnerable with you. Protect them by not interrupting and by instead empathizing. Do not feel the need to speak after each person shares. After most women have shared their answers to a question, turn it back to the Scripture from the study guide, and help them process the truth and hope in their struggles. Avoid lecturing, but do bring the women back to truth.

5. **Model trust:** Show them how you are applying these difficult lessons. Ask God to convict you and lead out with how you are processing change in your own life.

THE STUDY

This study is uniquely designed to work in any venue or location. I envision women leading this in their homes, on campuses, even in their workplaces. Church buildings are the traditional format for group Bible studies and *Get Out of Your Head* will be effective inside the church walls, but the bigger dream is that women would find this study useful in reaching their friends, neighbors, and coworkers.

Whether you find yourself with 150 women in a church auditorium or with a few neighbors in your living room, this study is designed for small groups of women to process truth within their souls. Because of the depth of the questions and topics, it is essential that your group be small enough to share. A maximum of eight women in each group is ideal, preferably fewer. If you are in a larger group, divide into smaller groups with volunteer facilitators. With the help of the leader's guide and the Ask conversation cards, those smaller groups should still prove successful with a little support.

SESSION FORMAT

This six-session study is designed to go deep very quickly. Since women are busy and have full lives, the beauty of this study is it can be led in a living room over a one-hour lunch, or in a church Bible study spread out over two and a half hours. If you have the flexibility, extend the time of sharing in small groups. A frequent complaint is, "We wish we had more time to share." When the group is given deep questions and space to reflect and respond, you'll be surprised how beautiful and plentiful the conversations will be.

These tools are meant to have some flexibility. Here are some suggestions for how to structure your meeting to get the most out of your time together. However, you will be the best judge of what works for your group and the time you have together. Based on your group's needs, choose any combination of going through the questions mixed with reflections from group members' personal study.

HOMEWORK DISCUSSION [10–25 MINUTES]:

After welcoming everyone and opening in prayer, you may choose to begin by having the women discuss their personal reflections as they have worked through the study guide and Scripture in the prior session. If you have more than eight members, break into small groups for this discussion time before reconvening for the video/teaching time.

VIDEO AND/OR TEACHING [15–18 MINUTES]:

Watch the DVD/video to provide a foundation for that session and to help transition to transparent sharing using the Ask conversation cards. If you are supplying teaching in addition to the videos, we recommend you begin with your teaching and then play the video.

ASK CONVERSATION CARDS [30–45 MINUTES]:

Especially if there are more than eight group members, divide into smaller groups and have women go through the Ask conversation cards (instructions on the next page). This will be a time of deep sharing and discussion that is important to learning how to apply all that has been studied that week.

SESSION TOOLS AND HOW TO USE THEM

See. The teaching videos are meant to set the tone for your time together, to draw women deeper into the Scripture, and to set the stage for transparent sharing. There is space in the study guide at the beginning of each week for taking notes during the video teaching. After Session 1, hopefully, each person has already studied the Scriptures for themselves before coming to the group, and the video will provide a jump-start to a powerful time of discussion and processing.

Ask. These cards provide a unique way of starting deep, honest conversations about our thought lives. Each session's cards are labeled with the appropriate session title. These should be pulled out after the video teaching time (DVD or streaming).

1. Lay out the cards for the session with the questions facing up.

2. Allow each woman to grab her favorite one.

3. Every week, go over the Ground Rules found in the front of the Ask deck of cards.

4. Begin by laying out the Scripture card for that session. Refer back to it as needed for help processing as you share.

5. Take turns having each woman ask the question on her card. Allow time for anyone who wants to share or respond to the question.

6. You may only get through a few of the questions. That is fine.

The goals of the questions are to allow women to reflect on what they have studied and heard and have a chance to share their own hearts. Again, allow everyone to concisely and clearly communicate their hearts, but always lead the discussion back to God and what Scripture offers in response that session's topic. Several of the cards each week have Scripture on them to help you do that. Pull one of those if you feel the group needs to hear what God says about the issues.

Study. In the first meeting, distribute your groups' study guides (or if women are purchasing on their own, remind them to bring their study guides to the first meeting). The sessions in the study guide (except for Session One) are meant to be completed during the week before coming to the group meeting. Each session in the guide begins with a short intro before moving into the portion marked Study. The Study portion is followed by four application projects, then closing thoughts from me. The Study portion and projects can be completed in one sitting or broken up into smaller parts throughout the week, depending on each individual woman's needs.

These sessions may feel different from studies you have done in the past. They are very interactive. The goal of the curriculum is to lead women to dig deeply into Scripture and uncover how it applies to their lives, to deeply engage the mind and the heart. Projects, stories, and Bible study all play a role. The projects in the study guide will provide several options for applying Scripture. You and your group members may be drawing or journaling or engaging in some other activity in these projects. At the group meeting discuss your experience in working through the lesson.

Lead. This guide serves as a tool to prepare you in leading this study and to encourage you along the way. Refer back to it each prior session to be aware of the goals for each one. The leader's guide will help you effectively point your women to the overarching theme of each session and point them to the themes of the study.

LEADING YOUR GROUP

TIPS AND THINGS TO WATCH OUT FOR

The study guide has the following information at the beginning. Review these guidelines carefully. During your first meeting, read through these expectations together as a group. Revisit these guidelines with the group in the coming weeks if necessary.

GET HONEST

This is going to get messy, but it will be worth it. We will be dealing with messy minds. God wants to do something about that. But until we recognize that we are fixing our minds on things other than Him, we will miss what He has for us. If you consider yourself out of control of your thoughts and feelings, perhaps you'll want to change that, even if it is costly. Be honest with yourself and honest with God. He knows all of it already, anyway.

ENGAGE WITH YOUR SMALL GROUP

Do not attempt to deal with such a large thing as the battle for your mind without kindred warriors at your side, fighting with you and for you. Pray, speak truth in love, and hold each other's feet to the fire. Be vulnerable and do not abandon those who are vulnerable with you. Prepare to go to war alongside these women. Keep your group in a safe place to wrestle and discover and also a place filled with truth. John described Christ as being "full of grace and truth" (John 1:14). I pray this is how your small group will also be described.

> And you will know the truth, and the truth will set you free (John 8:32).

Commit to be consistent and present. Every time you gather with your group you will be building your view of God and the way He built the workings of your mind. This study will create a circular understanding of God and His plan, and missing a week will leave a hole in that circle. Every time you are in your small group you will be processing God in your life. Consistency and presence show respect to God and those around you in this process.

Please be quick to listen and slow to speak. Lean into the Holy Spirit as you process together. Speak as He leads. This kind of vulnerable, Spirit-led communication with your group will help lead to lives that are running after the heart of God.

> Let every person be quick to hear, slow to speak (James 1:19).

GROUND RULES FOR GROUP DISCUSSION TIME

Be concise. Share your answers to the questions while protecting others' time for sharing. Be thoughtful. Don't be afraid to share with the group, but try not to dominate the conversation.

Keep group members' stories confidential. Many things your group members share are things they are choosing to share with you, not with your husband or other friends. Protect each other by not allowing anything shared in the group to leave the group.

Rely on Scripture for truth. We are prone to use conventional, worldly wisdom as truth. While there is value in that, this is not the place. If you feel led to respond, please only respond with God's truth and Word, not "advice."

No counseling. Protect the group by not directing all attention on solving one person's problem. This is the place for confessing and discovery and applying truth together as a group. Your group leader will be able to direct you to more help outside the group time if you need it. Don't be afraid to ask for help.

WHAT *GET OUT OF YOUR HEAD* IS NOT

Sidenote here:

I want to take a moment to acknowledge the truth and reality of mental illness. I've struggled through my own seasons of anxiety and depression and I know. And I'm sorry. I want to say that this study is going to speak of having power over our thoughts and minds, but there are some things we just don't have power over. Chemical imbalances are real and like cancer—you cannot just will yourself to not have cancer. Counseling and medicine can help. If you struggle with mental illness and need help, I encourage you to tell someone, ask, and find the help you need. I also think we all benefit from learning what we do have power over, what weapons we do have, and how we can stop spirals in our minds and take our thoughts captive.

GUIDING CONVERSATION

You may come across some challenges when leading a group conversation. Normally these fall into two categories. In both situations people will need encouragement and grace from you as a leader. As with everything in this study, seek the Holy Spirit's guidance as you interact with your group members.

1. Dominating the conversation: If one woman seems to be dominating the conversation or going into detail that makes the rest of the group uncomfortable, gently interrupt her if necessary and thank her for sharing. Avoid embarrassing her in front of the group. Ask if there is anyone else who would like to share in response to the original question

asked (not to necessarily respond to the woman who was just speaking). If the problem persists, talk with the woman outside of the group time. Affirm her for her vulnerability and willingness to share, and be prepared to refer her for more help if the need arises.

2. Not sharing as much as the others: If you notice there is a woman who seems to not be as talkative as the others in the group, you may try gently asking for her input directly at some point in the conversation. Some women are naturally shyer than others; don't try to force them into an extroverted role, but do let them know their input is valuable to the group. Remind them of the goals of the study and how being vulnerable with one another is one of the ways God shapes us spiritually. If a woman is just not interested in being in the study and is holding the rest of the group back, meet with her outside the group setting to discuss her further involvement.

Keep in mind that no two women are alike, but keep the best interests of the group in mind as you lead. For more information on two kinds of learners, see page 22.

WHEN TO REFER

Some of the women in your care may be suffering past the point you feel able to help. This study may bring the pain of adverse thoughts and emotions to the surface. To leave women in this state would be more damaging than helpful. Don't try to take on problems you do not feel equipped to handle. If you sense that a woman may need more help, follow up and refer her to someone.

Check with your church or pastor for names of trusted, certified Christian counselors. Some major indicators of this need would be: depression, anxiety, suicide, abuse, broken marriage. These are the obvious ones, but honestly, some women who are stuck in hurt from their past, minor depression, or fear could also benefit from counseling. I believe counseling is beneficial for many. So keep a stash of names for anyone you may feel needs to process further with a professional.

▶ Look for the nearest Celebrate Recovery group and offer to attend the first meeting with her (www.celebraterecovery.com).

▶ Suggest further resources and help to make a plan for their future growth and well-being.

▶ Communicate with the leadership at your church about how to proceed with care.

▶ Do not abandon these hurting women in a vulnerable place. This may be the first time they have opened up about painful hurts or patterns. Own their care and see it through. If they have landed in your group, God has assigned them to you for this season, until they are trusted to the care of someone else. Even then, continue to check in on them.

TYPES OF LEARNERS

Hopefully, you will be blessed to be leading this study with a group diverse in age, experience, and style. While the benefits of coming together as a diverse group to discuss God outweigh the challenges by a mile, there are often distinctions in learning styles. Just be aware and consider some of the differences in two types of learning styles that may be represented. (These are obviously generalizations, and each woman as an individual will express her own unique communication style, but in general these are common characteristics.)

EXPERIENTIAL LEARNERS

There are women who are more transparent, don't like anything cheesy, want to go deep quickly, and are passionate. Make a safe environment for them by being transparent yourself and engaging their hearts. These women may not care as much about head knowledge and may care more deeply how knowledge about God applies to their lives. They want to avoid being put in a box. Keep the focus on applying truth to their lives and they will stay engaged. Don't preach to them; be real and show them through your experiences how to pursue the mind of Christ.

PRAGMATIC LEARNERS

These women are more accustomed to a traditional, inductive, or precept approach to Bible study. They have a high value for truth and authority but may not place as high a value on the emotional aspects of confessing sin and being vulnerable. To them it may feel unnecessary or dramatic. Keep the focus on the truth of Scripture. These women keep truth in the forefront of their lives and play a valuable role in discipleship.

***

Because this study is different from traditional studies, some women may need more time to get used to the approach of this study. The goal is still to make God big in our lives, to fix our minds on Him, and to choose where to train our thoughts. We all just approach it in unique ways to reach unique types of people. I actually wrote this study praying it could reach both types of learners. I am one who lives with a foot in both worlds, trying to apply the deep truths I gained in seminary in an experiential way. I pray that this study would deeply engage the heart and the mind, and that we would be people who worship God in spirit and in truth, not just learning about the battle for our minds but going to war for them together

Common struggles like fear, stress, anger, shame, and insecurity are not respecters of age, religion, or income level. These struggles are human, and I have seen this study transcend the typical boundaries of Christian and seeker, young and old, single and married, needy and comfortable, bringing these women together and to God in a unique and powerful way.

In the following pages and notes for each session, I hope I have given you enough guidance that you do not feel lost, but enough freedom to depend on the Holy Spirit. These are only suggestions, but hopefully these notes will help surface themes and goals to guide you through your discussion of group members' homework and through the discussion of the Ask conversation cards. The video, homework, and cards should provide more than enough material for great discussions, but stay on track and be sure people are walking away with hope and truth.

INTRODUCTION

SPIRALING OUT

When we pay attention to what's going on in our heads, we realize we have a choice.

During this first meeting you will be getting to know each other, handing out the study guides, walking through the Instructions and Expectations (found on pp. 4–7 of the study guide), and watching the first video.

Here are some general goals and thoughts for your time together this week:

▶ Make the women feel safe.

▶ Get to know each other and the things you each struggle with.

▶ Set expectations for the study.

▶ Instruct group members on how to use the study guide, where to take notes from the video, and how you will use the Ask conversation cards.

▶ Create a need for this study in their lives by helping them see that we all are in a battle for our minds.

▶ Remind them that God is longing for a real relationship with each of us.

▶ Introduce the book of Philippians.

LEADER: This first session's suggested format is different from the others since it is your first meeting and there is no homework to review.

VIDEO TEACHING

For this first meeting, it is best to begin by watching the video session "Introduction: Spiraling Out." Remind women they can take notes from the teaching in their study guide to reference later in discussion or homework.

DISCUSSION TIME

1. Together take some time to read the Introduction, Instructions and Expectations, and the first session in the study guide either aloud or to yourselves and discuss.

2. When you reach page 21 in the first session of the study guide, have participants choose the ten things their minds are trained on most. Give everyone time to think about this, write down their answers in their guides, and fill out their mind maps.

3. If you are in a large group, break into small groups and give each person the chance to open up about their maps. Leaders, share first and be transparent.

4. After all the women have shared, you may transition to the Ask conversation cards to continue your discussion. The cards for this session are labeled "Introduction: Spiraling Out" on the front. Distribute the Ask cards and guide the women to ask and answer the questions on the cards. Review the Ask card instructions together. Remember to begin with the Scripture card and end by stressing the scriptural truth group members can apply to their lives as a result of what they

discussed in your group time. Close this discussion by praying for your coming weeks together and praising God for His Word and His unwavering love and pursuit of us.

> I have seen everything that is done under the sun, and behold, all is vanity and a striving after wind (Ecclesiastes 1:14).

MAKE THE SHIFT

MAIN IDEA

The mind of Christ is available to us—we just have to choose the direction of our thoughts.

In this session we will look at how we interrupt the spirals in our minds by making the shift up, toward God. We all have things we fixate on, and they can become idols if we make them our main focus. Paul cultivated the "mind of Christ" by making God the only and main thing. This is the starting point of our work and the only way it sticks. We have a choice to stop our spiraling thoughts, but we have to make the bigger choice first to point ourselves toward Him.

Here are some general goals and thoughts for your time together this week:

▶ Identify and define some of the things we fixate on to make us happy.

▶ Discover how Paul's calling was similar to God's calling for us.

▶ Discuss the things God says about who He is.

▶ A strong mind comes from surrender to God; we are not subject to our own thoughts and feelings but can make a choice to continually turn toward Him.

MAIN GOAL

Lead people to an honest evaluation of the source of their fixations, and encourage them to set their mind on the spirit.

HOMEWORK DISCUSSION

Suggestions on places to focus as you go over the homework with your group:

▶ Ask the group to share what they learned as they studied Paul in Philippians 1.

▶ Ask how Romans 8:5–11 speaks to them now in their lives.

▶ Discuss their response to Project 2.

▶ Ask what else they learned as they studied and interacted with the session and Scripture this week.

VIDEO TEACHING

Watch the video session "Make the Shift." Remind women they can take notes from the teaching in their study guide to reference later in discussion or homework.

ASK CONVERSATION CARDS

If you are in a large group, break into small groups for discussion time using the Ask conversation cards. Distribute this session's Ask cards and guide the women to ask and answer the questions on the cards. Remember to begin with the Scripture card and end by stressing the scriptural truth group members can apply to their lives as a result of what they discussed in your group time. Close this discussion by praying for the things shared and praising God for His position in our lives and in eternity.

"For who has understood the mind of the Lord so as to instruct him?" But we have the mind of Christ (1 Corinthians 2:16).

NOTES

WEAPONS WE USE

PART 1

MAIN IDEA

As we are developing the mind of Christ, we'll have a fight on our hands. But God gives us a weapon for every attack of the enemy.

Here are some general goals and thoughts for your time together this week:

▶ Create awareness of the way our inputs affect our attitudes.

▶ Create a dissatisfaction with the things the world throws at us to keep us distracted, like self-absorption, noise, and cynicism.

▶ What does it look like to live with humility? To be strengthened by silence? To welcome delight?

▶ The battle for the future is being fought between our ears; we participate in the renewal of our minds by filling them with the truth.

MAIN GOAL

Energize people to fight for their minds, encouraging them that renewal happens as we make choices for things of God rather than the distractions of the world.

HOMEWORK DISCUSSION

Suggestions on places to focus as you go over the homework with your group:

▶ Discuss their readings of Philippians 2.

▶ Which of the three spirals is most common for you?

- ▶ What was God speaking to you through Romans 12:1–2?

- ▶ Have women share their drawings from Project 2.

- ▶ Ask what else they learned as they studied and interacted with the lesson and Scripture this week.

VIDEO TEACHING

Watch the video session "Weapons We Use, Part I." Remind women they can take notes from the teaching in their study guide to reference later in discussion or homework.

ASK CONVERSATION CARDS

If you are in a large group, break into small groups for discussion time using the Ask conversation cards. Distribute this session's Ask cards and guide the women to ask and answer the questions on the cards. Remember to begin with the Scripture card and end by stressing the scriptural truth group members can apply to their lives as a result of what they discussed in your group time. Close this discussion by praying for the things shared and praising God for His position in our lives and in eternity.

> To the Jews who had believed him, Jesus said, "If you hold to my teaching, you are really my disciples. Then you will know the truth, and the truth will set you free" (John 8:31–32 NIV).

PART 2

MAIN IDEA

Our comfort zones can be dangerous places to dwell; God urges us out of them, toward connection, intentionality, and gratefulness.

Here are some general goals and thoughts for your time together this session:

▶ Help women to see that there are better options than victim mentality, complacency, and isolation.

▶ If we know God and trust Him we will obey no matter the cost, even if it feels uncomfortable.

▶ Every small shift toward service and connection makes a big impact on our minds.

▶ We weren't meant to be alone in the dark. God wants so much more for us, and for those He's put in our paths.

MAIN GOAL

Lead people to a right understanding of the gifts God gives us in community, in service, in gratefulness as they fight their spirals.

HOMEWORK DISCUSSION

Suggestions on places to focus as you go over the homework with your group:

What were the differences between Paul's approach to hardship and what we'd typically hear today?

- What did you feel as you reread Philippians 2?

- Which project stood out to you most this session?

- Ask what else they learned as they studied and interacted with the session and Scripture this week.

VIDEO TEACHING

Watch the video session "Weapons We Use, Part II." Remind women they can take notes from the teaching in their study guide to reference later in discussion or homework.

ASK CONVERSATION CARDS

If you are in a large group, break into small groups for discussion time using the Ask conversation cards. Distribute this session's Ask cards and guide the women to ask and answer the questions on the cards. Remember to begin with the Scripture card and end by stressing the scriptural truth group members can apply to their lives as a result of what they discussed in your group time. Close this discussion by praying for the things shared and praising God for His position in our lives and in eternity.

> Keep your heart with all vigilance, for from it flow the springs of life (Proverbs 4:23).

A NEW WAY TO LIVE

MAIN IDEA

As we develop the mind of Christ, we're growing in maturity. Once we leave our spirals and our past behind, we replace them with what we're running toward and growing into.

Here are some general goals and thoughts for your time together this session:

▶ Explain the concept of maturity according to Paul in Philippians 3.

▶ As someone with the mind of Christ, you'll never be at home in the darkness again. Forget what is behind and press on toward what is ahead for you.

▶ Once we've dumped the bondage, we have to replace it with something.

▶ Focus on the running, and our hindrances will fall off *as we run*.

▶ Freed people free people—we're a new creation with a job to do!

▶ We ask God for more faith. We go to Him with our doubts.

MAIN GOAL

Lead people to address the bondage of their past, bring it to God, and walk forward in maturity.

HOMEWORK DISCUSSION

Suggestions on places to focus as you go over the homework with your group:

▶ Talk about Paul's approach to "forgetting." Where did it come from?

▶ Discuss how that attitude would transform our lives today.

▶ Share your summaries of Philippians 3. What stood out most?

▶ Discuss the patterns in Project 3. Where do your women most desire to mature?

▶ Ask what else they learned as they studied and interacted with the session and Scripture this week

VIDEO TEACHING

Watch the video session "A New Way to Live." Remind women they can take notes from the teaching in their study guide to reference later in discussion or homework.

ASK CONVERSATION CARDS

If you are in a large group, break into small groups for discussion time using the Ask conversation cards. Distribute this session's Ask cards and guide the women to ask and answer the questions on the cards. Remember to begin with the Scripture card and end by stressing the scriptural truth group members can apply to their lives as a result of what they discussed in your group time. Close this discussion by praying for the things shared and praising God for His position in our lives and in eternity.

Indeed, I count everything as loss because of the surpassing worth of knowing Christ Jesus my Lord. For his sake I have suffered the loss of all things and count them as rubbish, in order that I may gain Christ and be found in him, not having a righteousness of my own that comes from the law, but that which comes through faith in Christ, the righteousness from God that depends on faith (Philippians 3:8-9).

NOTES

A MIND LIKE CHRIST

MAIN IDEA

The mind of Christ focuses on whatever is true, freed from lies and anxieties.

Here are some general goals and thoughts for your time together this session:

▶ Developing the mind of Christ is the project of a lifetime, but don't give up.

▶ God is with you in this war, as we learn to "think on these things."

▶ The lies we believe fall into three categories, but God gives us fundamental truths that will continue to set you free as you battle on into the future.

▶ Contentment is a result of a healthy mind. Walking with Jesus is the only thing that satisfies.

MAIN GOAL

Encourage people to keep fighting, to be honest about the lies they believe, and to hold fiercely to the truths God gives us.

HOMEWORK DISCUSSION

Suggestions on places to focus as you go over the homework with your group:

▶ What did you think of Paul's instruction to not be anxious about anything? How does that hit you?

▶ Discuss Paul's secret to contentment. How does this power us through our every day?

- Have women share their grids from Project 1.

- What are your reactions to 2 Corinthians 2:11–16?

- Ask what else they learned as they studied and interacted with the session and Scripture this week.

VIDEO TEACHING

Watch the video "A Mind Like Christ." Remind women they can take notes from the teaching in their study guide to reference later in discussion or homework

ASK CONVERSATION CARDS

If you are in a large group, break into small groups for discussion time using the Ask conversation cards. Distribute this session's Ask cards and guide the women to ask and answer the questions on the cards. Remember to begin with the Scripture card and end by stressing the scriptural truth group members can apply to their lives as a result of what they discussed in your group time. Close this discussion by praying for the things shared and praising God for His position in our lives and in eternity.

Finally, brothers, whatever is true, whatever is honorable, whatever is just, whatever is pure, whatever is lovely, whatever is commendable, if there is any excellence, if there is anything worthy of praise, think about these things. What you have learned and received and heard and seen in me—practice these things, and the God of peace will be with you (Philippians 4:8-9).

NOTES

You are in charge of your thoughts.
They are not in charge of you.

Get Out of Your Head: Stopping the Spiral of Toxic Thoughts is a Biblical guide to discovering how to submit our minds to Christ because how we think shapes how we live. As we surrender every thought to Jesus, the promises of God flood our lives in profound ways.

Visit **getoutofyourheadbook.com** for info about ***Get Out of Your Head.***

Available wherever books are sold.

Also Available from
jennie allen

Identify the threads of your life

In this DVD-based study using the story of Joseph, Jennie explains how his suffering, gifts, story, and relationships fit into the greater story of God— and how your story can do the same. She introduces Threads—a tool to help you see your own personal story and to uncover and understand the raw materials God has given you to use for his glory and purpose.

Visit **JennieAllen.com** for more info about *Restless*.

Available wherever books & Bibles are sold.

THOMAS NELSON
Since 1798

Also Available from
jennie allen

Chasing After the Heart of God

Chase is a Bible study experience to discover the heart of God and what it is exactly He wants from us. As we work through major events in the life of David, and the Psalms he wrote out of those experiences, you see a man who was reckless and imperfect but possessed the favor of God. Whether you are running from God or working your tail off to please Him, this man's journey will challenge your view of God.

Visit **JennieAllen.com** for more info about *Chase*.

Available wherever books & Bibles are sold.